DESIDERATA

ILLUSTRATIONS BY EMIL ANTONUCCI

a Brooke House book
distributed by Crown Publishers, Inc., New York

ISBN 0-517-53422-3

25   24   23

01326465

Go placidly

amid the noise & the haste,

& remember

what peace there may be in silence.

As far as possible without surrender

be on good terms with all persons.

Speak your truth

quietly & clearly; and listen to others, even to

the dull & the ignorant; they too have their story.

Avoid loud & aggressive persons,

they are vexatious to the spirit.

*If you compare yourself with others, you may
become vain or bitter; for always there will*

be greater & lesser persons than yourself.

Enjoy your achievements

as well as your plans.

Keep interested in your own career,
however humble;   it is a real possession

in the changing fortunes of time.

Exercise caution in your business affairs;

for the world is full of trickery.

But let not this blind you to what virtue

there is; many persons strive for high ideals;

and everywhere life is full of heroism.

Be yourself.

Especially, do not feign affection.

Neither be cynical about love;
for in the face of all aridity &

disenchantment it is as perennial as the grass.

Take kindly the counsel of the years,

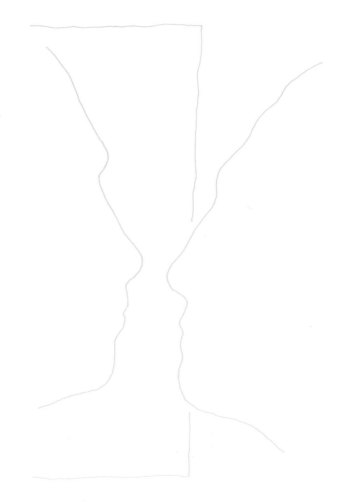

gracefully surrendering the things of youth.

Nurture strength of spirit to shield you

in sudden misfortune.

But do not distress yourself

with dark imaginings.

Many fears are born of fatigue & loneliness.

Beyond a wholesome discipline,

be gentle with yourself.

You are a child of the universe,
no less than the trees

& the stars; you have a right to be here.

And whether or not it is clear to you,

no doubt the universe is unfolding as it should.

Therefore be at peace with God,

whatever you conceive Him to be.

And whatever your

labors & aspirations, in the noisy

confusion of life keep peace in your soul.

With all its sham, drudgery

& broken dreams,

it is still a beautiful world.

Be cheerful.

Strive to be happy.

Desiderata, which is usually said to have been copied from an inscription "found in Old Saint Paul's Church, Baltimore; dated 1692," was actually written by an Indiana poet named Max Ehrmann and registered with the Copyright Office of the Library of Congress early in 1927. Copyright was renewed after the author's death by his widow, and the work still is protected by the United States Copyright Law. Thus, this popular philosophical statement is neither anonymous nor ancient, having both an author and a fairly recent date. Nonetheless, what it says remains timeless and reserves for its author a niche in that poetical pantheon to which belong those writers who have, at least once, seen an eternal truth clear.